My
Hollow
Home

Leanne Murner   Art by Vanessa Liebenberg

Serenity Press Pty Ltd
Waikiki, WA 6169

First published by Serenity Press (Serenity Press Kids) in 2022
www.serenitypress.org

National Library of Australia
Cataloguing-in-Publication entry

Murner, Leanne (Leanne, Murner), My Hollow Home

ISBN:

978-0-6482957-2-3
(Hardback)

978-0-6482957-6-1
(Paperback)

978-0-6482957-8-5
(Ebook)

I would like to dedicate this book to my husband and 5 boys. Thank you for all your support throughout this journey and being my inspiration to make a difference.

My
Hollow
Home

Leanne Murner

I am a gum tree, I am not like other trees. I am quite unique. I may look full and solid on the outside, but I can be hollow on the inside.

This is not the case with all eucalyptus trees. We start out as solid trees but if we have an injury, for example we get struck by lightning, then we become very vulnerable to white ants, or you may know them as termites.

These little insects will climb up to where we have an open wound and start feeding on our inner wood. This timber is dead and easy for them to consume. They will make a nest on one of our branches or the side of our trunk and start munching away at us.

This will hollow out our branches and trunk. The dead wood inside is not needed for us to be strong and to continue to grow. In fact, this can actually help us grow. The branch that fell will also be hollowed out, creating a habitat for ground wildlife, mammals, reptiles and insects. It can be used to build a nest, hide from larger prey or create a home.

My hardwood branches are used by Aboriginals to make their musical instruments, like the didgeridoo and clap sticks, as well as digging and hunting tools, like the woomera. The didgeridoos are made from one of my branches that they cut down or found on the ground.

Aboriginals can also use the bark of my tree to make shields and canoes. My leaves are used in cultural practices and burnt in smoking ceremonies.

I see all that happens on the ground around me, the little echidna hangs around the bottom of my trunk looking for food. They scratch and feed in the leaf litter and dirt around my roots. Echidnas love to eat ants, termites, worms, beetles and moth larvae.

Doing this also helps me survive. They loosen the ground underneath me, allowing air and water to come through so I can drink.

There is also another animal that hangs around down below digging and nibbling on my roots. Can you guess what it is?

It is the wombat. I am a great food source for the wombats. They like to dig around and nibble my roots. They do eat leaves and grasses as well, but they do not like gum leaves.

The wombat will not eat the leaves that have fallen from my tree to the ground. But that is okay.

My leaves fall to the ground and break down, creating plant food for the earth. It forms an insulation blanket from the heat, for the soil, in the warmer months and keeps the moisture in the ground, so it does not dry out.

My leaves are eaten by one important animal, do you know what that is?

It is the koala. But they do not eat all gum leaves. They only eat selected leaves from a range of trees. They are very picky when it comes to their food.

Koalas have big sharp claws and will climb up the side of my tree, sometimes leaving scratches on the bark.

The koala lives in my treetops and feeds and sleeps there. Did you know the koalas sleep for 18 to 22 hours a day, as they get very little energy from my leaves? Next time you see some scratches of the side of a eucalyptus tree, look up. You may see a koala in my treetop.

My leaves are also used in many other ways. When processed correctly they can be used for or made into herbal teas to treat colds and flu or processed into an oil for herbal use.

My bark has many functions. It helps protect the tree during bushfires. Some eucalyptus trees can shed their bark allowing new growth below.

It creates habitat for many critters, on and off the tree. Differences in my bark type is also a useful tool that can help to identify different species of gum trees.

Gum nuts and flowers are important parts of my tree. Some species of trees blossom over the warmer months, but other trees blossom over the cooler months. This assists in providing food all year round for the birds and bees.

Not many other flowers bloom over winter, and this would leave the birds and bees without food to survive.

Even with the wombat eating my roots, the koala eating my leaves and the white ants eating out the dead wood, I am still able to survive and produce growth.

There are many benefits to becoming hollow. It creates a safe space and homes for wildlife. I now have some hollow branches that the birds can nest in (called hollow nesting). These hollow nests protect the young from prey like eagles and goannas.

Possums will live in my trunk. They will sleep all day and are active at night.

There is another very small little creature only weighing 150g that nests in my hollow logs or small crevices in my bark. Can you guess what it is?

It is the microbat. These little creatures love to sleep all day and feed on insects all night. Even though they are so small, they can consume 40% of their body weight in insects in a single night. That can be 700 insects per hour.

With my tree full of white ants and the nest on the side of my tree they do not need to go far for a feast.

There is another little important insect that will create a wild nest out of wax and resin in my tree.

Have you heard of a sugarbag bee? They are a very small stingless bee measuring 3 to 5mm and are dark in colour.

Each hive produces only small amounts of honey, less than 1kg per year.

These bees are not like honey bees, they store the honey and pollen to provide food over the cooler months to rear the larvae.

Having all these animals and insects living inside my branches and trunk helps me survive.

All their waste, droppings and seeds drop to the bottom of my trunk to feed my roots. My roots grow in search of nutrients to help me survive. Even though the width of my root zone grows at least twice the height of my trunk, and with a whole ecosystem happening inside me, this can also cause my roots to turn and grow back into the centre of my tree to feed on all these nutrients.

Ecology is the study of the home, I have shared my
life as just one tree on the land and how important we
are. I have shared how all things are related and work
together to support life for the ecosystem: forests,
plants and animals and other organisms in the soil.
This can help educate tomorrow's decision-makers
to help our planet to support life and to teach you to
leave a bit for the bush.

EUCALYPTUS / GUM TREE

These trees can grow to great height and age. There are over 700 species of this tree and the leaves, bark and flowers differ across them all. They are an amazing food source for nectar birds, pollinators and insects. The oil from the leaves is used in medicines and aromatic purposes.

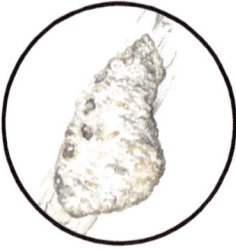

WHITE ANT / TERMITE

There are around 360 species of termites in Australia, but only a small number cause economic damage to crops, timber and buildings. Most termites are of great benefit to ecosystems through recycling dead and rotten timber and other plant matter and as a source of food to many animals.

ECHIDNA

The echidna is one of 3 egg-laying mammals in the world and can live up to 45 years.

Echidnas have toothless jaws, so they use their snouts and claws to tear open logs, then use their 15cm long tongues and pads on the roof of their mouths to break down their food.

WOMBAT

Wombats are short-legged, muscular marsupials that are native to Australia. A fully grown adult can be up to 1m in length and weigh 20 to 35 kg.

They dig extensive burrows with their rodent-like front teeth and powerful claws. One distinctive adaptation of wombats is their backward pouch. The advantage of a backward-facing pouch is that when digging, they do not gather soil in their pouch over their young.

KOALA

Koalas survive on a diet of eucalyptus leaves and can eat up to a kilogram a day. Pretty impressive, considering eucalyptus is poisonous to most animals. However, they are quite picky, and only eat less than 50 of the 700 eucalyptus species.

They can sleep up to 18 hours a day because their bodies need a lot of energy to digest the gum leaves.

Sadly, koala numbers have been falling further and further every year due to deforestation, fire and disease. These struggling species have now been pushed even further towards the brink of extinction.

MICROBAT

Microbats see with their ears rather than their eyes. They produce a sound and 'listen' for it as it bounces back from surrounding objects. When cruising, microbats emit about 10 pulses per second. When an insect is detected, the pulses go up to over 100 per second.

During summer and autumn, microbats go into a feeding frenzy as they fatten up on insects to help them survive the winter. Adult microbats feed on lawn grub moths, weevils, caterpillars, beetles, midges, flying termites, mosquitoes and other insects. Microbats can eat as much as 40% of their own body weight in a single night or several hundred insects per hour.

SUGARBAG BEE

These bees are about 3 to 5mm in length.

Each nest has a queen, drones and thousands of workers. These bees produce sugarbag honey, a highly prized food of Aboriginals who gather it from wild nests. Each hive produces less than 1kg of honey per year so it is a special product, to be savoured and relished.

GALAH

The galah can be easily identified by its rose-pink head, neck and underparts, with paler pink crown, and grey back, wings and undertail.

Huge noisy flocks of birds congregate and roost together at night. The flocks feed on seeds, mostly from the ground.

Female galahs will lay 4 to 6 eggs in her tree hollow but unfortunately only half will usually survive. However, once the chicks make it to adulthood, they will usually live for about 25 years in the wild or up to 80 years when kept as pets. Like other cockatoos, the galah is an excellent mimic of voices and sounds.

RAINBOW LORIKEET

These birds have bright red beaks that really stand out from their bluish-purple heads. Their wings, back and tail are all bright green, and their chests are an orangish-yellow. These colourful birds like to live near coastal areas and make their nests in hollow branches of eucalyptus trees.

They have a special tongue that is covered in little hairs that help the birds dig out pollen and nectar from flowers.

COCKATOO

There are 21 different species of cockatoo in Australia, each with a unique look and colour. All cockatoos are sociable and enjoy hanging out in large groups. Some can live for 50 to 80 years.

They feed on seeds of grasses, trees and grain crops. They also eat berries, nuts and leaf buds, and some insects and their larvae. Their strong beaks and tongues are well-adapted for this diet.

KOOKABURRA

Although kookaburras are known for being an Australian bird, only the blue-winged and laugh-ing kookaburras are found in Australia. The other two species are also found in New Guinea.

Kookaburras are carnivorous and will eat insects, small mammals, lizards and even venomous snakes.

Their distinctive 'laughs' are used to mark and protect their territory.

COMMON BRUSHTAIL POSSUM

The largest of the possums, brushtails can be identi-fied by their silvery-grey colour, a band across their nose, pointy ears, and of course, their bushy tail.

Possums prefer to reside in tree hollows, but many animals, birds and insects of both the native and non-native variety want to live in them too. As more mature trees get cut down,there are less and less natural homes for possums and other creatures.

Their main predators include dingoes, pythons, foxes and cats. Brushtail possums only come out at night when they go in search of food. They like to feed on eucalyptus as well as a range of other leaves, berries and fruit.

www.ingramcontent.com/pod-product-compliance
Lightning Source LLC
Chambersburg PA
CBHW040748150426
42811CB00060B/1530